## The Early Church Today Series

## ST. CLEMENT OF ALEXANDRIA

# WHO IS THE RICH MAN THAT SHALL BE SAVED?

## THE EARLY CHURCH TODAY SERIES

Volume 7

The early leaders of the Church, tasked with shepherding Christ's flock, left us spiritual wealth that is too often neglected in modern times. The Early Church Today Series, published by the St. Mary & St. Moses Abbey Press, aims to help make that richness more accessible to readers, inviting them to see the applicability of the early Church to our walk with God today. By sharing practical selections from the writings of the early Church, aided by meaningful editorial supplements and revisions, each book will attempt to diminish impediments and bring to light what the Church has to offer.

ST. MARY & MOSES ABBEY PRESS

# WHO IS THE RICH MAN THAT SHALL BE SAVED?

## ST. CLEMENT OF ALEXANDRIA

Translation by

## G.W. Butterworth

ST MARY & MOSES ABBEY PRESS

Who is the Rich Man That Shall be Saved?

By St. Clement of Alexandria

Translation by G.W. Butterworth

Minor editing of the original translation was done by St. Mary and St. Moses Abbey, mainly changing archaic words to their modern counterparts. The text was retrieved from: *Clement of Alexandria*, Butterworth G.W., trans. (New York, NY: The Loeb Classical Library, 1919).

Designed & Published by:
St. Mary & St. Moses Abbey Press
101 S Vista Dr, Sandia, TX 78383
stmabbeypress.com

Cover Icon of St. Clement was written by Mina Anton.

# CONTENTS

# INTRODUCTION

## Who is St. Clement of Alexandria?

Titus Flavius Clement was a Church Father, born around AD 150. He was originally a pagan philosopher, who travelled extensively through many lands in search of knowledge and teachers, including Greece, Italy, Palestine, Egypt. And he met many "blessed and truly remarkable men,"[1] as he says. Upon meeting Pantaenus, the head of the Catechetical School at Alexandria, he stopped his pursuits and became his disciple. Of Pantaenus, he says:

> When I came upon the last (he was the first in power), having tracked him out concealed in Egypt, I found rest. He, the true, the Sicilian bee, gathering the spoil of the flowers of the prophetic and apostolic meadow, engendered in the souls of his hearers a deathless element of knowledge.[2]

---

1    Clement of Alexandria, *Stomata* 1. (ANF[2]).
2    Ibid.

St. Clement succeeded Pantaenus as the head of Catechetical School at Alexandria, and the Church was illumined by his teaching. Alexander, Bishop of Jerusalem, who was one of St. Clement's disciples, said after the latter's repose, "For we know well those blessed fathers who have trodden the way before us, with whom we shall soon be; Pantaenus, the truly blessed man and master, and the holy Clement, my master and benefactor, and if there is any other like them, through whom I became acquainted with you, the best in everything, my master and brother."[3] The scholar Origen was also a disciple of his. St. Cyril of Alexandria says that he was "a man admirably learned and skillful, and one that searched to the depths all the learning of the Greeks, with an exactness rarely attained before."[4] Also St. Jerome wrote about him saying, "Clement, a presbyter of Alexandria, in my judgment the most learned of men, wrote eight books of *Miscellanies* and as many of *Outline Sketches*, a treatise against the Gentiles, and three volumes called the *Pedagogue*. Is there any want of learning in these, or are they not rather drawn from the very heart of philosophy?"[5] He is thought to have passed away about AD 220.

---

3    Eusebius, *The Church History* 6.14. (NPNF[2] 1).
4    Clement of Alexandria, *Stomata* 1. (ANF[2]).
5    Jerome, *Letters* LXX. (NPNF[2] 6).

WHO IS THE RICH MAN

THAT SHALL BE SAVED?

## The Sin of Flattering Rich Men

1. Men who offer laudatory speeches as presents to the rich may rightly be classed, in my opinion, not only as flatterers and servile, since in the hope of a large return they make a show of granting favors that are really no favors, but also as impious and insidious. They are impious, because, while neglecting to praise and glorify the only perfect and good God, from whom are all things and through whom are all things and to whom are all things,[6] they invest with His prerogative men who are wallowing in a riotous and filthy life and, in short, are lying under the judgment of God. They are insidious, because, although mere abundance is by itself quite enough to puff up the souls of its possessors, and to corrupt them, and to turn them aside from the way by which salvation can be reached, these men bring fresh delusion to the minds of the rich by exciting them with the pleasures that come from their immoderate praises, and by rendering them contemptuous of absolutely everything in the world except the wealth which is the cause of their being admired. In the words of the proverb, they carry fire to fire, when they shower pride upon pride, and heap on wealth, heavy by its own nature, the heavier burden of arrogance. Rather they ought to have diminished and curtailed wealth, as a perilous and deadly disease; for the man who exalts and magnifies himself is in danger of a complete reversal of fortune, namely, the change and fall into low estate, as the divine word teaches.[7] It seems to

---

6    Romans 11:36.
7    Matthew 23:12.

me an act far kinder than servile attention to the rich and praise that does them harm, if we share the burden of their life and work out salvation for them by every possible means; first by begging them from God, who unfailingly and gladly accords such gifts to His own children, and then by healing their souls with reason, through the Savior's grace, enlightening them and leading them on to the possession of the truth. For only he who has reached the truth and is distinguished in good works shall carry off the prize of eternal life. But prayer requires a soul that runs its course strong and persevering until the last day of life, and the Christian citizenship requires a disposition that is good and steadfast and that strains to fulfill all the Savior's commandments.

## Reasons Why Salvation Seems Difficult for Rich Men

2. Now the reason why salvation seems to be more difficult for the rich than for men without wealth is probably not a simple one, but complex. For some, after merely listening in an off-hand way to the Lord's saying, that a camel shall more easily creep through a needle's eye than a rich man into the kingdom of heaven,[8] despair of themselves, feeling that they are not destined to obtain life. So, complying with the world in everything, and clinging to this present life as the only one left to them, they depart further from the heavenward way, taking no more trouble to ask who are the rich men that the Master and Teacher is addressing

---

8    Mark 10:25.

nor how that which is impossible with men becomes possible. Others however understand the saying rightly and properly, but, because they make light of the works which bear upon salvation, do not provide the necessary preparation for the satisfaction of their hopes. In both cases I am speaking of the rich who have learnt of the Savior's power and His splendid salvation; with those who are uninitiated in the truth I have little concern.

### Christians Must Show Them That Salvation is not Impossible, But Effort is Necessary

3. It is the duty, therefore, of those whose minds are set on love of truth and love of the brethren, and who neither behave with insolent rudeness towards the rich members of the church, nor yet flatter them through personal love of gain, first, by means of the word of scripture, to banish from them their unfounded despair and to show, with the necessary exposition of the Lord's oracles, that the inheritance of the kingdom of heaven is not completely cut off from them, if they obey the commandments; and afterwards, when they have learnt that their fears are groundless, and that the Savior gladly receives them if they desire, to point out and instruct them how and through what kind of works and resolves they can enjoy the object of their hope, which is neither beyond their reach nor, on the contrary, to be obtained without settled purpose. Well then, as is the case with athletes—if we may compare things small and perishable with things great and incorruptible— so let him who is rich in this world consider it to be with

himself. For the athlete who has no hope of being able to win and to obtain crowns does not even enroll himself for the contest; while the one who at heart entertains this hope, but does not submit to hard training and exercises and suitable food, comes out uncrowned and entirely misses the fulfilment of his hopes. In the same way let not one who is clothed with this earthly covering[9] proclaim himself barred at the start from the Savior's prizes, if, that is, he is faithful and surveys the magnificence of God's love to men; nor, once again, let him hope, by remaining undisciplined and unused to conflict, to partake of the crowns of incorruption without dust and sweat. But let him come and subject himself to reason as trainer and to Christ as master of the contests. Let his appointed food and drink be the Lord's new covenant,[10] his exercise the commandments, his grace and adornment the fair virtues of love, faith, hope,[11] knowledge of the truth, goodness, gentleness, compassion, gravity; in order that, when the last trumpet[12] signals the end of the race and his departure from the present life as from a course, he may with a good conscience stand before the judge a victor, admitted to be worthy of the fatherland above, into which with angelic crowns and proclamations he now ascends.[13]

---

9    I.e., riches.

10    See 1 Corinthians 11:25.

11    See 1 Corinthians 13:13.

12    See 1 Corinthians 15:52.

13    The imagery in this fine passage is taken from the Greek games, which St. Paul also had used as an illustration of the spiritual conflict. See 1 Corinthians 9:25.

## A Prayer for the Savior's Help

4. May the Savior grant us power, then, as we begin our address at this point, to impart to the brethren true and fitting and salutary thoughts, first with regard to the hope itself, and secondly with regard to the means of reaching it. He gives freely to those who need, and teaches them when they ask, and disperses their ignorance, and shakes off their despair, by bringing up again the self-same words about the rich and showing them to be their own sure interpreters and expositors. For there is nothing like hearing once more the actual sayings which, because in our childishness we listened to them uncritically and mistakenly, have continued until now to trouble us in the gospels.

## The Gospel Passage About the Rich Man

As He was going forth into the way, one came and kneeled before Him, saying, "Good Master, what shall I do that I may inherit eternal life." And Jesus says, "Why do you call Me good? None is good save one, that is, God. You know the commandments; do not commit adultery, do not kill, do not steal, do not bear false witness, honor your father and mother." And he answering says to Him, "All these things have I observed from my youth." And Jesus looking upon him loved him, and said, "One thing you lack. If you want to be perfect, sell whatsoever you have and distribute to the poor, and you shall have treasure in heaven;

and come, follow Me." But his countenance fell at the saying, and he went away sorrowful; for he was one that had great riches and lands. And Jesus looked round about, and says to His disciples, "How hardly shall they that have riches enter into the kingdom of God!" And the disciples were amazed at His words. But Jesus answering again says to them, "Children, how hard is it for them that trust in riches to enter into the kingdom of God! A camel shall more easily enter through the eye of the needle, than a rich man into the kingdom of God." And they were exceedingly astonished and said, "Who then can be saved?" But He looking upon them said, "That which is impossible with men is possible with God." Peter began to say to him, "Lo, we have left all and followed You." And Jesus answering says, "Verily I say to you, whoever leaves his home and parents and brothers and riches for My sake and for the gospel's sake, shall receive back a hundredfold. To what end is it that in this present time we have lands and riches and houses and brothers with persecutions? But in the time to come is life eternal. The first shall be last and the last first."[14]

---

14    Mark 10:17–31. It will be noticed that the text of St. Mark's gospel used by Clement differed in a number of small points from that with which we are familiar.

## The Passage Must not be Interpreted in a Merely Literal Sense

5. This is written in the gospel according to Mark, and in all the other accepted gospels the passage as a whole shows the same general sense, though perhaps here and there a little of the wording changes. And as we are clearly aware that the Savior teaches His people nothing in a merely human way, but everything by a divine and mystical wisdom, we must not understand His words literally, but with due inquiry and intelligence we must search out and master their hidden meaning. For the sayings which appear to have been simplified by the Lord Himself to His disciples are found even now, on account of the extraordinary degree of wisdom in them, to need not less but more attention than His dark and suggestive utterances. And when the sayings which are thought to have been fully explained by Him to the inner circle of disciples, to the very men who are called by Him the children of the kingdom,[15] still require further reflection, surely those that had the appearance of being delivered in simple form and for that reason were not questioned by the hearers, but which are of importance for the whole end of salvation, and are enveloped in a wonderful and super-celestial depth of thought, should not be taken as they strike the careless ear, but with an effort of mind to reach the very spirit of the Savior and His secret meaning.

---

15   Matthew 13:38.

## The Rich Man's Quesetion was Appropriate to Our Lord

6. For our Lord and Savior is pleased to be asked a question most appropriate to Him; the Life is asked about life, the Savior about salvation, the Teacher about the chief of the doctrines He was teaching, the Truth about the true immortality, the Word about the Father's word, the perfect One about the perfect rest, the incorruptible about the sure incorruption. He is asked about the things for which He has even come to earth, and which are the objects of His training, His teaching, His bounty; in order that He may reveal the purpose of the gospel, that it is a gift of eternal life. As God He knows before-hand both what questions He will be asked and what answers will be given Him. For who should know this more than the Prophet of prophets and the Lord of every prophetic spirit? And when He is called good, He takes His keynote from this very first word and makes it the starting-point of His teaching, turning the disciple to God who is good, and first of all, and alone dispenser of eternal life, which the Son gives to us after receiving it from Him.[16]

## The First of All Doctrines: to Know God

7. We must therefore store up in the soul right from the beginning the greatest and chiefest of the doctrines that refer to life, namely, to know the eternal God as both giver of eternal gifts and first and supreme and one

---

16  See John 5:26; 17:2.

and a good God.[17] And we can get possession of God through knowledge and apprehension; for this is a firm and unshakable beginning and foundation of life,— the knowledge of God who truly exists and who is the bestower of things that exist, that is, of eternal things, from whom it is that the rest of things take both their existence and their continuance. Ignorance of Him is death, but full knowledge of Him, and close friendship, and love to Him, and growth in His likeness, is alone life.

## Then to Know the Savior

8. He therefore that aims at living the true life is bidden first to know Him whom "no man knows except the Son, and he to whomsoever the Son reveals Him"[18]: and then to understand the Savior's greatness, next to Him, and the newness of His grace; because, according to the apostle, "the law was given through Moses, grace and truth through Jesus Christ,"[19] and gifts given through a faithful slave[20] are not equal to those bestowed by a true son. At any rate, if the law of Moses was able to supply eternal life, it is in vain that the Savior comes Himself to us and suffers on our account,[21] running His human course from birth to the cross; in vain, too, that he who has kept "from youth" all the commandments of Moses' law kneels and asks immortality from another. For not only has he fulfilled the law, but he

---

17    See John 17:3.

18    Matthew 11:27.

19    John 1:17.

20    The reference is to Moses in Hebrews 3:5.

21    See Galatians 2:21.

began to do so right from his earliest years. For what is there great or especially distinguished about an old age free from the brood of sins that are born of youthful lusts or boiling anger or passion for riches? But if a man in the heyday and heat of youth displays a ripe spirit older than his years, he is a wonderful and illustrious champion and gray-haired in judgment. Nevertheless the young man in question is positively convinced that while, as regards righteousness, nothing is lacking to him, life is lacking altogether. So he asks it from Him who alone is able to give it. As regards the law, too, he speaks with boldness, but to the Son of God he makes supplication. He passes over "from faith to faith."[22] As he tosses perilously in the dangerous roadstead of the law he is brought to a safe anchorage with the Savior.

## The Rich Man was Still Imperfect

9. Certainly Jesus does not convict him of not having fulfilled all the demands of the law. No, He loves him and warmly welcomes him for his ready obedience in what he has learned. Yet He calls him imperfect as regards eternal life, on the ground that he has fulfilled deeds that are not perfect, and that though he is a worker of the law, he is idle in respect of true life. Now the works of the law are good— who will deny it? for "the commandment is holy,"[23]—but only to the extent of being a kind of training, accompanied by fear and preparatory instruction, leading on to the supreme lawgiving and grace of Jesus.[24] On the other hand

22    Romans 1:17.

23    Romans 12:12.

24    See Galatians 3:24.

"Christ is the fulfilment of the law unto righteousness to everyone that believes,"[25] and those who perfectly observe the Father's will He makes not slaves, in the manner of a slave,[26] but sons and brothers and joint-heirs.[27]

## The Rich Man was Free to Choose Life

10. "If you want to become perfect."[28] So he was not yet perfect; for there are no degrees of perfection. And the "if you want to" was a divine declaration of the free-will of the soul that was talking with Him. For the choice lay with the man as a free being, though the gift was with God as Lord. And He gives to those who desire and are in deep earnest and beg, that in this way salvation may become their very own. For God does not compel, since force is hateful to God, but He provides for those who seek, He supplies to those who ask, and He opens to those who knock.[29] If you want to, then, if you really want to and are not deceiving yourself, get possession of that which is wanting. "One thing you lack,"[30] the one thing, that which is Mine, the good, that which is already above law, which law does not give, which law does not contain, which is peculiar to those who live. Yet indeed he who has fulfilled every demand of the law "from youth" and has made extravagant boasts, is unable to add to the tale this one thing singled

25    Romans 10:4, and 13:10.

26    I.e. Moses; cp. Hebrews 3:5–6.

27    See Matthew 12:50, and Romans 8:14–17.

28    Matthew 19:21.

29    See Matthew 7:7, and Luke 11:9.

30    Mark 10:21; Luke 18:22.

out by the Savior, in order to obtain the eternal life which he longs for. He went away displeased, being annoyed at the precept concerning the life for which he was making supplication. For he did not truly wish for life, as he said, but aimed solely at a reputation for good intentions. He could be busy about many things, but the one thing, the work that brings life, he was neither able nor eager nor strong enough to accomplish. And just as the Savior said to Martha when she was busy about many things, distracted and troubled by serving, and chiding her sister because she had left the household work and was seated at His feet spending her time in learning: "You are troubled about many things, but Mary has chosen the good part, and it shall not be taken away from her,"[31]—so also He bade this man cease from his manifold activities and cling to and sit beside one thing, the grace of Him who adds eternal life.

## The Meaning of the Command: "Sell What Belongs to You"

11. What then was it that impelled him to flight, and made him desert his teacher, his supplication, his hope, his life, his previous labors? "Sell what belongs to you."[32] And what is this? It is not what some hastily take it to be, a command to fling away the substance that belongs to him and to part with his riches, but to banish from the soul its opinions about riches, its attachment to them, its excessive desire, its morbid excitement over them, its anxious cares,

---

31    Luke 10:38–42.
32    Matthew 19:21; Mark 10:21.

the thorns of our earthly existence which choke the seed of the true life.[33] For it is no great or enviable thing to be simply without riches, apart from the purpose of obtaining life. Why, if this were so, those men who have nothing at all, but are destitute and beg for their daily bread, who lie along the roads in abject poverty, would, though "ignorant" of God and "God's righteousness,"[34] be most blessed and beloved of God and the only possessors of eternal life, by the sole fact of their being utterly without ways and means of livelihood and in want of the smallest necessities. Nor again is it a new thing to renounce wealth and give it freely to the poor, or to one's fatherland, which many have done before the Savior's coming, some to obtain leisure for letters and for dead wisdom, others for empty fame and vainglory—such men as Anaxagoras, Democritus and Crates.

## The Command Means to Strip the Soul of its Passions

12. What then is it that He enjoins as new and peculiar to God and alone life-giving, which did not save men of former days? If the "new creation,"[35] the Son of God, reveals and teaches something unique, then His command does not refer to the visible act, the very thing that others

---

33    The allusion is to the parable of the Sower.

34    Romans 10:3.

35    The Greek words ἡ καινὴ κτίσις according to Segaar mean: "a creature to whom nothing has ever existed on earth equal or like, man but also God, through whom is true light and everlasting life." [See footnote in Clement of Alexandria, *Who is the Rich Man That Shall be Saved*. (ANF²)]

have done, but to something else greater, more divine and more perfect, which is signified through this; namely, to strip the soul itself and the will of their lurking passions and utterly to root out and cast away all alien thoughts from the mind. For this is a lesson peculiar to the believer and a doctrine worthy of the Savior. The men of former days, indeed, in their contempt for outward things, parted with and sacrificed their possessions, but as for the passions of the soul, I think they even intensified them. For they became supercilious, boastful, conceited and disdainful of the rest of mankind, as if they themselves had accomplished something superhuman. How then could the Savior have recommended to those who were to live forever things that would be harmful and injurious for the life He promises? And there is this other point. It is possible for a man, after having unburdened himself of his property, to be none the less continually absorbed and occupied in the desire and longing for it. He has given up the use of wealth, but now being in difficulties and at the same time yearning after what he threw away, he endures a double annoyance, the absence of means of support[36] and the presence of regret. For when a man lacks the necessities of life he cannot possibly fail to be broken in spirit and to neglect the higher things, as he strives to procure these necessities by any means and from any source.

---

36    Strictly, service rendered by rowers on a ship, in relation to the work of sailors and pilot; hence, services rendered by wealth, etc., for the support and comfort of life.

## Those Only Who Have Money Can Obey Other Commands of the Lord

13. And how much more useful is the opposite condition, when by possessing a sufficiency, a man is himself in no distress about money-making and also helps those he ought? For what sharing would be left among men, if nobody had anything? And how could this doctrine be found other than plainly contradictory to and at war with many other noble doctrines of the Lord? "Make to yourselves friends from the mammon of unrighteousness, that when it shall fail, they may receive you into the eternal habitations."[37] "Acquire treasures in heaven, where neither moth nor rust consumes, nor thieves break through."[38] How could we feed the hungry and give drink to the thirsty, cover the naked and entertain the homeless, with regard to which deeds He threatens fire and the outer darkness to those who have not done them,[39] if each of us were himself already in want of all these things? But further, the Lord Himself is a guest with Zacchaeus[40] and Levi and Matthew,[41] wealthy men and tax-gatherers, and He does not bid them give up their riches. On the contrary, having enjoined the just and set aside the unjust employment of them, He proclaims, "Today is salvation come to this house."[42] It is on this condition that He praises their use,

---

37  Luke 16:9.
38  Matthew 6:20.
39  See Matthew 25:41–43.
40  See Luke 19:5.
41  See Mark 2:15.
42  Luke 19:9.

and with this stipulation,—that He commands them to be shared, to give drink to the thirsty and bread to the hungry, to receive the homeless, to clothe the naked. And if it is not possible to satisfy these needs except with riches, and He were bidding us stand aloof from riches, what else would the Lord be doing than exhorting us to give and also not to give the same things, to feed and not to feed, to receive and to shut out, to share and not to share? But this would be the height of unreason.

## Riches are to be Used for the Good of Others

14. We must not then fling away the riches that are of benefit to our neighbors as well as ourselves. For they are called possessions because they are things possessed, and wealth because they are to be welcomed and because they have been prepared by God for the welfare of men. Indeed, they lie at hand and are put at our disposal as a sort of material and as instruments to be well used by those who know. An instrument, if you use it with artistic skill, is a thing of art; but if you are lacking in skill, it reaps the benefit of your unmusical nature, though not itself responsible. Wealth too is an instrument of the same kind. You can use it rightly; it ministers to righteousness. But if one uses it wrongly, it is found to be a minister of wrong. For its nature is to minister, not to rule. We must not therefore put the responsibility on that which, having in itself neither good nor evil, is not responsible, but on that which has the power of using things either well or badly, as a result of choice; for this is responsible just for that reason.

And this is the mind of man, which has in itself both free judgment and full liberty to deal with what is given to it. So let a man do away, not with his possessions, but rather with the passions of his soul, which do not consent to the better use of what he has; in order that, by becoming noble and good, he may be able to use these possessions also in a noble manner. "Saying good-bye to all we have,"[43] and "selling all we have,"[44] must therefore be understood in this way, as spoken with reference to the soul's passions.

## Outward Things are Indifferernt

15. I for my part would put the matter thus. Since possessions of one kind are within the soul, and those of another kind outside it, and these latter appear to be good if the soul uses them well, but bad if they are badly used, which of the two is it that He, who orders us to get rid of what we have, asks us to renounce? Is it those after whose removal the passions still remain, or rather those after whose removal even outward possessions become useful? He who has cast away his worldly abundance can still be rich in passions even though his substance is gone. For his disposition continues its own activity, choking and stifling the power of reasoning and inflaming him with its inbred desires. It has proved no great gain then for him to be poor in possessions when he is rich in passions. For he has cast away not the worthless things but the indifferent, and while depriving himself of what is serviceable he has set on fire the innate material of

---

43    See Luke 14:33.
44    See Matthew 19:21.

evil by the lack of outward things. A man must say good-bye, then, to the injurious things he has, not to those that can actually contribute to his advantage if he knows the right use of them; and advantage comes from those that are managed with wisdom, moderation and piety. We must reject what is hurtful; but outward things are not injurious.

## Poverty of Passions is Needed

In this way then the Lord admits the use of outward things, bidding us put away, not the means of living, but the things that use these badly; and these are, as we have seen, the infirmities and passions of the soul. 16. Wealth of these brings death whenever it is present, but salvation when it is destroyed. Of this wealth a man must render his soul pure, that is, poor and bare, and then only must he listen to the Savior when He says, "Come, follow Me."[45] For He Himself now becomes a way to the pure in heart;[46] but into an impure soul God's grace does not move. An impure soul is that which is rich in lusts and in travail with many worldly affections. For he who holds possessions and gold and silver and houses as gifts of God, and from them ministers to the salvation of men for God the giver, and knows that he possesses them for his brothers' sakes rather than his own, and lives superior to the possession of them; who is not the slave of his possessions, and does not carry them about in his soul, nor limit and circumscribe his own life in them, but is ever striving to do some noble and

---

45    Mark 10:21.

46    See John 14:6; Matthew 5:8.

divine deed; and who, if he is fated ever to be deprived of them, is able to bear their loss with a cheerful mind exactly as he bore their abundance—this is the man who is blessed by the Lord and called poor in spirit,[47] a ready inheritor of the kingdom of heaven, not a rich man who cannot obtain life.

## Wealth in the Soul Shuts Out From Heaven

17. But he who carries his wealth in his soul, and in place of God's Spirit carries in his heart gold or an estate, who is always extending his possession without limit, and is continually on the lookout for more, whose eyes are turned downwards and who is fettered by the snares of the world, who is earth and destined to return to earth?[48]—how can he desire and meditate on the kingdom of heaven? A man that bears about not a heart, but an estate or a mine, will he not necessarily be found among these things on which he fixed his choice? "For where the mind of a man is, there is his treasure also."[49]

## Two Kinds of Treasures and Two Kinds of Wealth and Poverty

Now as for treasures, the Lord knows them to be of two kinds, one good, for "the good man out of the good treasure of the heart brings forth that which is good"; and the other

---

47    Matthew 5:3.

48    See Genesis 3:19.

49    See Matthew 6:21; Luke 12:34.

bad, for "the evil man out of his evil treasure brings forth that which is evil, because out of the abundance of the heart the mouth speaks."[50] As therefore treasure is, with Him as with us, not single only, there being that kind which brings great and immediate gain in the finding, but a second kind also that is without gain, unenviable, undesirable and harmful, so also there is one wealth of good things, another of evil; since we know that wealth and treasure are not by nature separate from each other. And the one kind of wealth would be desirable and worth getting; the other undesirable and worthless. In the same manner also poverty is blessed, that is, the spiritual kind. Therefore Matthew added to "Blessed are the poor"; how? "in spirit."[51] And again, "Blessed are they that hunger and thirst after God's righteousness."[52] Those then who are poor in the opposite sense[53] are miserable, being destitute of God, more destitute still of human possessions, and unacquainted with God's righteousness.

## Spiritual Meanings of "Rich" and "Poor"

18. So with regard to the rich, who shall hardly enter into the kingdom, we must understand the word in the spirit of disciples, and not clumsily, rudely, or literally; for it is not spoken thus. Salvation does not depend upon outward things, whether they are many or few, small or great, splendid

50    Luke 6:45.

51    Matthew 5:3.

52    Matthew 5:6.

53    I.e., those who possess no money, and do not hunger after righteousness.

or lowly, glorious or mean, but upon the soul's virtue, upon faith, hope, love, brotherliness, knowledge, gentleness, humility and truth, of which salvation is the prize. For a man will not obtain life on account of bodily beauty, nor perish for want of it; but he who uses holily and according to God's will the body that was given him shall obtain life, and he who destroys the temple of God shall be destroyed.[54] It is possible for a man, though ugly, to be licentious, and in beauty to be chaste. Strength and greatness of body do not give life, nor does insignificance of the limbs destroy, but the soul by its use of these provides the cause that leads to either result. Accordingly the scripture says, "When you are struck, offer your face,"[55] which a man can obey even though he is strong and in good health; whereas one who is weakly can transgress through an uncontrolled temper. Thus a man without means of livelihood might perhaps be found drunk with lusts, and one rich in possessions sober and poor as regards pleasures, believing, prudent, pure, disciplined. If then it is first and foremost the soul which is destined to live, and virtue growing in the soul saves it while evil kills, it is at once abundantly clear that the soul is being saved when it is poor in those things by wealth of which a man is destroyed, and that it is being killed when it is rich in those things a wealth of which brings ruin. So let us no longer seek for the cause of our end anywhere else except in the character and disposition of the soul with regard to its obedience to God and its purity, to its transgression of commandments and accumulation of evil.

---

54   See 1 Corinthians 3:17.
55   See Matthew 5:39; Luke 6:29.

## How the Rich Man Must Sell His Possessions

19. The man who is truly and nobly rich, then, is he who is rich in virtues and able to use every fortune in a holy and faithful manner; but the spurious rich man is he who is rich according to the flesh, and has changed his life into outward possessions which are passing away and perishing, belonging now to one, now to another, and in the end to no one at all. Again, in the same way there is a genuine poor man and also a spurious and falsely-named poor man, the one poor in spirit, the inner personal poverty, and the other poor in worldly goods, the outward alien poverty. Now to him who is not poor in worldly goods and is rich in passions the man who is poor in spirit and is rich towards God says, "Detach yourself from the alien possessions that dwell in your soul, in order that you may become pure in heart and may see God,[56] which in other words means to enter into the kingdom of heaven. And how are you to detach yourself from them? By selling them. What then? Are you to take riches for possessions, to make an exchange of one wealth for another by turning real estate into money? Not at all. But in place of that which formerly dwelt in the soul you long to save, bring in another kind of wealth that makes you divine and provides eternal life, namely, resolves that are fixed in accord with God's commandment; and in return for these you shall have abundant reward and honor, perpetual salvation and eternal incorruption. In this way you make a good sale of what you have, of the many things that are superfluous

---

56    Matthew 5:8.

and that shut heaven against you, while you receive in exchange for them the things that have power to save. As for the first, let the fleshly poor who need them have them; but you, having received in their stead the spiritual wealth, will now have treasure in heaven."[57]

## The Rich Man Misunderstood Christ's Command

20. The very rich and law-abiding man, not understanding these things correctly, nor how the same man can be both poor and wealthy, can have riches and not have them, can use the world and not use it, went away gloomy and downcast. He abandoned the rank of that life which he could desire indeed, but could not attain to; since what was hard he himself had made impossible. For it was hard to prevent the soul being led away and dazzled by the luxuries and splendid allurements that are associated with visible wealth, yet it was not impossible even amid this to lay hold of salvation, if one would but transfer himself from the sensible wealth to that which belongs to the mind and is taught by God, and would learn to make good and proper use of things indifferent and how to set out for eternal life. Even the disciples themselves are at first filled with fear and amazement. For what reason do you think? Was it because they too possessed great riches? Why, their very nets and hooks and fishing-boats they had left long ago, and these were all they had. Why then do they say in fear, "Who can be saved?"[58] It was because they

---

57    Mark 10:21.
58    Mark 10:26,

understood well and as disciples should that which was spoken in dark parables by the Lord, and perceived the depth of His words. As far as lack of riches and possessions went they had good hopes for salvation, but since they were conscious that they had not yet completely put away their passions—for they were fresh disciples and but lately enlisted by the Savior—"they were exceedingly amazed,"[59] and began to despair of themselves no less than did that very rich man who clung desperately to his possession, which indeed he preferred to eternal life. It was then for the disciples an altogether fit occasion for fear, if both the possessor of outward wealth and also he who carries a brood of passions—in which even they were rich—are equally to be banished from heaven. For salvation belongs to pure and passionless souls.

## God Helps Those Who Earnestly Desire Life

21. But the Lord answers: "that which is impossible with men is possible for God."[60] This again is full of great wisdom, because when practicing and striving after the passionless state by himself man achieves nothing, but if he makes it clear that he is eagerly pursuing this aim and is in deep earnest, he prevails by the addition of the power that comes from God. For God breathes His own power into souls when they desire, but if ever they desist from their eagerness, then too the spirit given from God is withdrawn; for to save men against their will is an act

---

59    Ibid.

60    Mark 10:27.

of force, but to save them when they choose is an act of grace. Nor does the kingdom of God belong to sleepers and sluggards, but "the men of force seize it."[61] This is the only good force, to force God and to seize life from God; and He, knowing those who forcibly, or rather persistently, cling to Him, yields; for God welcomes being worsted in such contests. Therefore on hearing these things the blessed Peter, the chosen, the pre-eminent, the first of the disciples, on behalf of whom alone and Himself the Savior pays the tribute,[62] quickly seized upon and understood the saying. And what does he say? "Lo, we have left all and followed You."[63] If by "all" he means his own possessions, he is bragging of having forsaken four obols or so, as the saying goes, and he would be unconsciously declaring the kingdom of heaven a suitable equivalent to these. But if, as we are just now saying, it is by flinging away the old possessions of the mind and diseases of the soul that they are following in the track of their teacher, Peter's words would at once apply to those who are to be enrolled in heaven.[64] For this is the true following of the Savior, when we seek after His sinlessness and perfection, adorning and regulating the soul before Him as before a mirror and arranging it in every detail after His likeness.

---

61 Matthew 11:12.

62 See Matthew 17:27.

63 Mark 10:28.

64 See Luke 10:20; Hebrews 12:23.

## The Meaning of Christ's Command
## to Leave Parents and Kinsfolk

22. And Jesus answered, "Verily I say to you, whoever leaves his home and parents and brothers and riches for My sake and for the gospel's sake shall receive back a hundredfold."[65] Let not this saying however disturb us, nor yet the still harder one uttered elsewhere in the words, "He that hates not father and mother and children, yes and his own life also, cannot be My disciple."[66] For the God of peace, who exhorts us to love even our enemies, does not propose that we should hate and part from our dearest ones. If a man must love his enemies, he must also by the same rule, reasoning upward from them, love his nearest of kin. Or if he must hate his blood relations, much more does reason, by a downward process, teach him to abhor his enemies; so that the sayings would be proved to cancel one another. But they do not cancel one another, nor anything like it; for from the same mind and disposition, and with the same end in view, a man may hate a father and love an enemy, if he neither takes vengeance on his enemy nor honors his father more than Christ. For in the one saying Christ cuts at the root of hatred and evil-doing, in the other of false respect for our kindred, if they do us harm as regards salvation. If, for instance, a man had a godless father or son or brother, who became a hindrance to his faith and an obstacle to the life above, let him not live in fellowship or agreement with him, but let him dissolve the fleshly relationship on account of the spiritual antagonism.

65    Mark 10:29.
66    Luke 14:26.

## The Appeal of Earthly Kindred and of Christ

23. Think of the matter as a lawsuit. Imagine your father standing by you and saying, "I begot you and brought you up, follow me, take part in my wrong-doing and do not obey the law of Christ," and whatever else a man who was a blasphemer and in nature dead might say. But from the other side hear the Savior; "I gave you new birth,[67] when by the world you were evilly born for death; I set you free, I healed you, I redeemed you. I will provide you with a life unending, eternal, above the world. I will show you the face of God the good Father.[68] 'Call no man your father upon earth.'[69] 'Let the dead bury their dead, but do you follow Me.'[70] For I will lead you up to a rest and to an enjoyment of unspeakable and indescribable good things 'which eye has not seen nor ear heard, nor have they entered into the heart of man, which angels desire to look into and to see what good things God has prepared for His saints and for His children that love Him.'[71] I am your nurse, giving Myself for bread, which none who taste have any longer trial of death,[72] and giving day by day drink of immortality.[73] I am a teacher of heavenly instructions. On your behalf I wrestled with death and paid your penalty of death, which you owed for your former sins and your faithlessness towards God."

---

67  See 1 Peter 1:3.

68  See John 14:8–9.

69  Matthew 23:9.

70  Matthew 8:22.

71  See 1 Corinthians 2:9; 1 Peter 1:12.

72  See John 6:50–51; Hebrews 11:36.

73  See John 4:14.

When you have listened to these appeals from each side pass judgment on your own behalf and cast the vote for your own salvation. Even though a brother says the like, or a child or wife or anyone else, before all let it be Christ that conquers in you; since it is on your behalf He struggles.

## Salvation Must Come Before All Else

24. Can you also rise superior to your riches? Say so, and Christ does not draw you away from the possession of them; the Lord does not grudge. But do you see yourself being worsted and overthrown by them? Leave them, cast them off, hate them, say good-bye to them, flee from them. "And if your right eye causes you to stumble, quickly cut it out." Better the kingdom of God with one eye, than the fire with both. And if it be a hand or a foot or your life, hate it. For if here it perishes for Christ's sake, there it shall be saved.[74]

## The Meaning of "With Persecutions"

25. This meaning attaches likewise to the passage which follows. "To what end is it that in this present time we have lands and riches and houses and brothers with persecutions?"[75] For it is not simply men without riches or homes or brothers that He calls to life, since He has also called rich men (though in the sense we have before stated); and brothers likewise, as Peter with Andrew, and James with John, the sons of Zebedee, though these were brothers of one mind with each other and with Christ. But

74  See Matthew 5:29–30; 18:8; and Mark 9:43–47.
75  Mark 10:30.

He disapproves of our having each of these things "with persecutions." Now one kind of persecution comes from without, when men, whether through hatred, or envy, or love of gain, or by the prompting of the devil, harry the faithful. But the hardest persecution is that from within, proceeding from each man's soul that is defiled by godless lusts and manifold pleasures, by low hopes and corrupting imaginations; when, ever coveting more, and maddened and inflamed by fierce loves, it is stung by its attendant passions, as by goads or a gad-fly, into states of frenzied excitement, into despair of life and contempt of God. This persecution is heavier and harder, because it arises from within and is ever with us; nor can the victim escape from it, for he carries his enemy about within himself everywhere. So too with regard to burning; that which falls on us from without effects a testing, but that from within works death. And war also; that which is brought against us is easily ended, but war in the soul accompanies us till death. If joined with such persecution you have visible wealth and brothers by blood and all the other separable possessions, abandon your sole enjoyment of these which leads to evil, grant to yourself peace, become free from a persecution that lasts, turn away from them to the gospel, choose before all the Savior, the advocate and counsel for your soul, the president of the infinite life. "For the things that are seen are temporal, but the things that are not seen are eternal";[76] and in the present time things are fleeting and uncertain, but "in the world to come is life eternal."[77]

---

76     2 Corinthians 4:18.

77     Mark 10:30:

## Salvation is Possible if Rich Men Obey God

26. "The first shall be last and the last first."[78] This saying, though fruitful in its deeper meaning and interpretation, does not call for examination at the present time, for it applies not merely to those who have great possessions, but generally to all men who once devote themselves to faith. So for the time being let it be reserved. But as to the question before us, I think it has been shown that the promise[79] does not fall short in any respect, because the Savior has by no means shut out the rich, at any rate so far as their actual riches and investments of property are concerned, nor has He trenched off salvation from them, provided they are able and willing to stoop beneath God's commandments and that they value their own life above temporal things and look to the Lord with steadfast gaze, like sailors on the watch for the nod of a good pilot to see what are his wishes, his commands, his signals, what watchword he gives them, where and whence he proclaims the harbor. For what wrong does a man do, if by careful thought and frugality he has before his conversion gathered enough to live on; or, what is still less open to censure, if from the very first he was placed by God, the distributor of fortune, in a household of such men, in a family abounding in riches and powerful in wealth? For if he has been banished from life for being born, through no choice of his own, in wealth, it is rather he who is wronged by God who brought him into existence, seeing that he has been counted worthy of temporal comfort, but deprived of eternal life. Why would wealth ever have arisen

78    Mark 10:31.
79    I.e., the gospel promise of salvation for all men.

40

at all out of earth, if it is the provider and agent of death? But if a man can keep within bounds the power that possessions bring, and can be modest in thought and self-controlled, seeking God alone, living in an atmosphere of God and as a fellow-citizen with God, here is one who approaches the commandments as a poor man, as free, unconquered, untouched by the diseases or wounds of riches. If not, a camel shall more quickly enter through a needle than shall such a rich man reach the kingdom of God.[80] Now the camel, that passes through a strait and narrow way[81] sooner than the rich man, must be understood to have some higher meaning, which, as a mystery of the Savior, can be learnt in my *Exposition concerning First Principles and Theology.* 27. Here, however, let me set forth the first and obvious meaning of the illustration, and the reason why it was used. Let it teach the well-to-do that their salvation must not be neglected on the ground that they are already condemned beforehand, nor on the contrary must they throw their wealth overboard or give judgment against it as insidious and inimical to life, but they must learn how and in what manner wealth is to be used and life acquired. For since a man is neither absolutely being lost if he is rich but fearful, nor absolutely being saved because he is bold and confident that he will be saved, let us now go on to inquire what hope it is that the Savior outlines for the rich, and how the unhoped for may become secure, and the hoped for pass into possession.

---

80   Mark 10:25.
81   Matthew 7:14.

## The First and Greatest Commandment

When asked which is the greatest of the commandments the Teacher says, "You shall love the Lord your God with all your soul and with all your power," and that there is no commandment greater than this[82]—and quite naturally. For indeed it is a precept concerning the first and the greatest existence, God Himself our Father, through whom all things have come into being and exist, and to whom the things that are being saved return again.[83] As therefore we were first loved by Him[84] and took our beginning from Him, it is not reverent to consider any other thing as more venerable or more honorable. This is the only thanks we pay Him, a small return for the greatest blessings; and we are not able to think of the slightest thing else to serve as recompense for a God who is perfect and in need of nothing. But by the very act of loving the Father to the limit of our personal strength and power we gain incorruption. For in proportion as a man loves God, he enters more closely into God.

## The Second Great Commandment

28. Second in order, and in no way less important than this, is, He says, the commandment, "You shall love your neighbor as yourself"[85]—God therefore you must love more than yourself. And when His questioner inquires,

---

82   Mark 12:30–31.

83   See Romans 11:36.

84   See 1 John 4:19.

85   Luke 10:27.

"Who is a neighbor?"[86] He did not point, in the same way as the Jews did, to their blood-relation, or fellow-citizen, or proselyte, or to the man who like them was circumcised, or to a keeper of one and the same law, but He describes a man going down from Jerusalem to Jericho,[87] showing him stabbed by robbers and flung half dead upon the road. A priest passes him by; a Levite disregards him; but he is pitied by the scorned and outcast Samaritan, who did not pass along by chance[88] as the others, but had come fully equipped with what the man in danger needed, wine, oil, bandages, a beast, and payment for the innkeeper, some being given there and then and a further amount promised. "Which of these," He said, "proved neighbor to him who endured this outrage?" And when he answered, "He that showed pity towards him," the Lord added, "Go therefore and do likewise." For love bursts forth into good works.

## Jesus Christ is Our Nearest Neighbor

29. In both commandments therefore He introduces love, but He makes a distinction of order, in one place attaching to God the highest exercise of love and in the other allotting its secondary exercise to our neighbor. And who else can this be but the Savior Himself? Or who more than He has pitied us, who have been almost done to death by the world-rulers of the darkness[89] with these many wounds—

---

86   Luke 10:29.
87   See Luke 10:30–37.
88   See Luke 10:31.
89   Ephesians 6:12.

with fears, lusts, wraths, griefs, deceits and pleasures? Of these wounds Jesus is the only healer, by cutting out the passions absolutely and from the very root. He does not deal with the bare results, the fruits of bad plants, as the law did, but brings His axe to the roots of evil.[90] This is He who poured over our wounded souls the wine, the blood of David's vine; this is He who has brought and is lavishing on us the oil, the oil of pity from the Father's heart; this is He who has shown us the unbreakable bands of health and salvation, love, faith and hope;[91] this is He who has ordered angels and principalities and powers[92] to serve us for great reward, because they too shall be freed from the vanity of the world at the revelation of the glory of the sons of God.[93] Him therefore we must love equally with God. And he loves Christ Jesus who does His will and keeps His commandments.[94] "For not everyone that says unto Me, 'Lord, Lord,' shall enter into the kingdom of heaven, but he that does the will of My Father."[95] And, "Why do you call Me, 'Lord, Lord,' and do not do the things that I say?"[96] And "Blessed are you that see and hear what neither righteous men nor prophets saw and heard," if you do what I say.[97]

---

90   See Matthew 3:10; Luke 3:9.

91   1 Corinthians 13:13.

92   See Hebrews 1:14; Ephesians 3:10.

93   See Romans 8:19–21.

94   See John 14:15.

95   Matthew 7:21.

96   Luke 6:46.

97   See Matthew 13:16–17; John 13:17.

## Next We Must Love Christ's Brethren

30. He then is first who loves Christ, and the second is he who honors and respects those who believe on Christ. For whatever service a man does for a disciple the Lord accepts for Himself, and reckons it all His own. "'Come, you blessed of My Father, inherit the kingdom prepared for you from the foundation of the world. For I was hungry and you gave Me to eat, and I was thirsty and you gave Me to drink, and I was a stranger and you took Me in, I was naked and you clothed Me, I was sick and you visited Me, I was in prison and you came unto Me.' Then shall the righteous answer Him saying, 'Lord, when did we see You hungry and fed You, or thirsty and gave You drink? When did we see You a stranger and took You in, or naked and clothed You? Or when did we see You sick and visited You? Or in prison and came unto You?' The King shall answer and say unto them, 'Verily I say unto you, inasmuch as you did it unto one of these My brethren, even these least, you did it unto Me.'"[98] Again, on the other hand, those who did not provide these things for them He casts into the eternal fire, on the ground that they have not provided them for Him. And in another place: "He that receives you receives Me; he that does not receive you rejects Me."[99]

## Names of Love and Honor for Christ's Disciples

31. These who believe on Him He calls children and young

---

98    Matthew 25:34–40.
99    See Matthew 10:40; Luke 10:16.

children and babes and friends;[100] also little ones here,[101] in comparison with their future greatness above. "Despise not," He says, "one of the little ones, for their angels always behold the face of My Father who is in heaven."[102] And elsewhere: "Fear not, little flock, for it is the Father's good pleasure to give you the kingdom"[103] of heaven. After the same manner He says that the least in the kingdom of heaven, that is, His own disciple, is greater than the greatest among them that are born of women, namely John.[104] And again, "He that receives a righteous man or a prophet shall obtain the reward fit for these, and he that has given a cup of cold water to a disciple in the name of a disciple shall not lose his reward."[105] This then is the only reward that cannot be lost. And once more: "Make to yourselves friends from the mammon of unrighteousness, that when it shall fail, they may receive you into the eternal habitations."[106] Thus He declares that all possessions are by nature unrighteous, when a man possesses them for personal advantage as being entirely his own,[107] and does not bring them into the common stock for those in need; but that from this unrighteousness it is possible to perform a deed that is righteous and saving, namely, to give relief to one of those who have an eternal habitation with the Father.

---

100  See Mark 10:24; John 21:5, 15:15; Matthew 11:25; Luke 12:4.

101  See Matthew 10:42.

102  Matthew 18:10.

103  Luke 12:32.

104  See Matthew 11:11; Luke 7:28.

105  Matthew 10:41–42.

106  Luke 16:9.

107  The phrase comes from Acts 4:32.

## The Great Reward of Service
## to Christ's Disciples

See, first, how His command is not that you should yield to a request or wait to be pestered, but that you should personally seek out men whom you may benefit, men who are worthy disciples of the Savior. Now the Apostle's saying also is good, "God loves a cheerful giver,"[108] one who takes pleasure in giving and sows not sparingly, for fear he should reap sparingly,[109] but shares his goods without murmurings or dispute or annoyance. This is sincere kindness. Better than this is that which is said by the Lord in another place: "Give to everyone that asks you";[110] for such generosity is truly of God. But more divine than all is this saying, that we should not even wait to be asked, but should personally seek after whoever is worthy of help, and then fix the exceedingly great reward of our sharing, an eternal habitation. 32. What splendid trading! What divine business! You buy incorruption with money. You give the perishing things of the world and receive in exchange for them an eternal abode in heaven. Set sail, rich man, for this market, if you are wise. Go around the whole earth if need be. Spare not dangers or toils, that here you may buy a heavenly kingdom. Why so delighted with glittering stones and emeralds, with a house that is fuel for fire or a plaything for time or sport for an earthquake or the object of a tyrant's insolence? Desire to live and reign in heaven with God. This kingdom a man,

---

108   2 Corinthians 9:7.

109   See 2 Corinthians 9:6.

110   Luke 6:30.

imitating God, shall give you. Having taken little from you here, he will make you through all the ages a fellow-inhabitant there. Beg him to take it. Hasten, strive earnestly, fear lest he reject you. For he has not been commanded to take, but you to provide. Furthermore, the Lord did not say, "give." or "provide," or "benefit," or "help," but "make a friend";[111] and a friend is made not from one gift, but from complete relief and long companionship. For neither faith nor love nor patience is the work of one day, but "he that endures to the end, the same shall be saved."[112]

## Do Not Distinguish Between the "Worthy" and "Unworthy"

33. How then does a man give these things? Why, the Lord gives them, on account of your esteem and favor and relationship with this man. "For I will give not only to my friends, but also to the friends of my friends." And who is this friend of God? Do not yourself decide who is worthy and who unworthy, for you may happen to be quite mistaken in your opinion; so that when in doubt through ignorance it is better to do good even to the unworthy for the sake of the worthy than by being on your guard against the less good not to light upon the virtuous at all. For by being miserly and by pretending to test who will deserve the benefit and who will not, you may possibly neglect some who are beloved of God, the penalty for which is eternal punishment by fire. But by giving freely to all in turn who

111  Luke 16:9.
112  Matthew 10:22.

need, you are absolutely certain to find one of those men who have power to save you with God. Therefore, "judge not, that you may not be judged; with what measure you use,[113] it shall be measured to you again. Good measure, pressed down and shaken together, running over, shall be given back to you."[114] Open your heart to all who are enrolled as God's disciples, not gazing scornfully on their body, nor being led to indifference by their age. And if one appear needy or ill-clad or ungainly or weak, do not in your soul take offence at this and turn away. This is a form thrown round us from without for the purpose of our entrance into the world, that we may be able to take our place in this universal school; but hidden within dwells the Father, and His Son[115] who died for us and rose with us.

## The Real Wealth and Beauty are Within

34. This form that is seen deceives death and the devil; for the inward wealth and beauty are invisible to them. And they rage round the bit of flesh, which they despise as weak, while they are blind to the inner possessions, not knowing how great a "treasure" we carry "in an earthen vessel,"[116] fortified by the power of God the Father and the blood of God the Son and the dew of the Holy Spirit. Do not be deceived, however, you who have tasted of truth, and have been deemed worthy of the great redemption; but, contrary to the rest of men, enlist on your behalf an army without

---

113  Original translation: "mete" instead of "use."

114  See Matthew 7:1; Luke 6:38.

115  See John 14:23.

116  2 Corinthians 4:7.

weapons, without war, without bloodshed, without anger, without stain, an army of God-fearing old men, of God-beloved orphans, of widows armed with gentleness, of men adorned with love. Obtain with your wealth, as guards for your body and your soul, such men as these, whose commander is God. Through them the sinking ship rises, steered by the prayers of saints alone; and sickness at its height is subdued, put to flight by the laying on of hands; the attack of robbers is made harmless, being stripped of its weapons by pious prayers; and the violence of demons is shattered, reduced to impotence by confident commands.

## The Many Services the Saints Can Render

35. Effective soldiers are all these, and steadfast guardians, not one idle, not one useless. One is able to beg your life from God, another to cheer you up when sick, another to weep and lament in sympathy on your behalf before the Lord of all, another to teach some part of what is useful for salvation, another to give outspoken warning, another friendly counsel, and all to love you truly, without guile, fear, hypocrisy, flattery or pretense. What sweet services of loving friends! What blessed ministries of men of good cheer! What pure faith of those who fear God alone! What truth of speech among those who cannot lie! What beauty of deeds among those who are resolved to minister to God, to persuade God, to please God! They seem to touch not your flesh but each his own soul, not to be talking with a brother but with the King of the ages[117] who dwells in you.

---

117   1 Timothy 1:17.

## The Highest Grade of the Elect

36. All the faithful then are noble and godlike, and worthy of their title, which they wear as a diadem. Not but that there are already some who are even more elect than the elect, and more elect in proportion as they are less conspicuous. These are they who in a manner haul themselves up out of the surf of the world and retire to a place of safety, who do not wish to appear holy, and are ashamed if one calls them so, who hide in the depth of their mind the unutterable mysteries, and scorn to let their nobility of nature be seen in the world. These the Word calls "light of the world" and "salt of the earth."[118] This is the seed, God's image and likeness, and His true child and heir,[119] sent here, as it were, on a kind of foreign service by the Father's high dispensation and suitable choice. For his sake both the visible and invisible things of the world have been created, some for his service, others for his training, others for his instruction; and all are held together so long as the seed remains on earth, and when it has been gathered in, all will speedily be dissolved.

## God is Love

37. What else is necessary? Behold the mysteries of love, and then you will have a vision of the bosom of the Father, whom the only-begotten God alone declared.[120] God

---

118   Matthew 5:13–14.

119   See Genesis 1:26; Romans 8:17; 1 Timothy 1:2; Titus 1:4.

120   John 1:18.

in His very self is love,[121] and for love's sake He became visible to us. And while the unspeakable part of Him is Father, the part that has sympathy with us is Mother.[122] By His loving the Father became of woman's nature, a great proof of which is He whom He begat from Himself; and the fruit that is born of love is love. This is why the Son Himself came to earth, this is why He put on manhood, this is why He willingly endured man's lot, that, having been measured to the weakness of us whom He loved, He might in return measure us to His own power. And when He is about to be offered[123] and is giving Himself up as a ransom He leaves us a new testament: "I give you my love."[124] What love is this, and how great? On behalf of each of us He laid down the life that is equal in value to the whole world. In return He demands this sacrifice from us on behalf of one another. But if we owe our lives to the brethren, and admit such a reciprocal compact with the Savior, shall we still be frugal with and hoard up the things of the world, which are beggarly and alien to us and ever slipping away? Shall we shut out from one another that which in a short time the fire will have? Divine indeed and inspired is the saying of John: "He that loves not his brother is a murderer,"[125] a seed of Cain, a nursling of the devil. He has no tender heart of God, no hope of better

---

121  See 1 John 4:8, 16.

122  Clement is simply trying to account, in a mystical way, for the love of God as shown in the Incarnation. [Translator's note].

123  I.e., as a drink-offering—the same word that St. Paul uses of himself in 2 Timothy 4:6.

124  See John 13:34; 14:27.

125  1 John 3:15.

things. He is without seed and without offspring. He is no branch of the ever-living heavenly vine. He is cut off; he awaits the fire at once.[126]

## Love with True Repentance
## Gains God's Forgiveness

38. But do learn the "more excellent way"[127] to salvation, which Paul shows. "Love does not seek its own,"[128] but is lavished upon the brother. For him love flutters with excitement, for him it is chastely wild. "Love covers a multitude of sins. Perfect love casts out fear. Love does not parade itself, is not puffed up, does not rejoice in unrighteousness, but rejoices with the truth; bears all things, believes all things, hopes all things, endures all things. Love never fails; prophecies are done away, tongues cease, healings are left behind on earth; but these three remain, faith, hope, love; and the greatest among these is love."[129] And rightly; for faith departs, when we believe through having seen God with our own eyes; and hope vanishes away when what we hoped for has been granted; but love goes with us into the fullness of God's presence and increases the more when that which is perfect has been bestowed. Even though a man be born in sins, and have done many of the deeds that are forbidden, if he but implant love in his soul he is able, by increasing the love

---

126  See John 15:5–6.

127  1 Corinthians 12:31.

128  1 Corinthians 13:5.

129  See 1 Peter 4:8; 1 John 4:18; 1 Corinthians 13:4–13.

and by accepting pure repentance, to retrieve his failures. For if you understand who is the rich man that has no place in heaven, and also in what manner a man may so use his substance (39) as to win his way to life through the censure and difficulties caused by wealth, and to be able to enjoy the eternal good things,—yes, even though he has happened either because of ignorance or of weakness or of circumstances not of his own choice to fall after the baptismal seal and redemption into certain sins or transgressions so as to have become completely subject to them,—let not this thought remain with you to lead to despair and despondency, namely, that such an one has been condemned outright by God. For to everyone who turns to God in truth with his whole heart the doors are opened and a thrice-glad Father receives a truly penitent son. And genuine repentance is to be no longer guilty of the same offences, but utterly to root out of the soul the sins for which a man condemned himself to death; because when these have been destroyed God will once again enter in and dwell with you. For He says that there is great and unsurpassable joy and feasting in heaven for the Father and the angels when one sinner has turned and repented.[130] Accordingly He cries, "I wish for mercy and not sacrifice, I desire not the death of the sinner, but his repentance. Though your sins be as scarlet wool, I will whiten them as snow; though blacker than the darkness, I will wash them and make them as white wool."[131] For God alone can grant

---

130   See Luke 15:7, 10.
131   See Matthew 9:13; 12:7 (from Hosea 6:6); Ezekiel 18:23; Isaiah 1:18.

remission of sins and not reckon trespasses,[132] though even we are exhorted by the Lord each day to forgive our brothers when they repent.[133] And if we, being evil, know how to give good gifts,[134] how much more does "the Father of mercies."[135] The good Father "of all comfort,"[136] full of pity[137] and full of mercy, is by nature long-suffering. He waits for those who turn to Him. And to turn to Him truly is to cease from sins and no more to look back.[138]

## Repentance Means a Complete Change of Life

40. Of sins already committed, then, God gives remission, but of those that are to come each man procures his own remission. And this is repentance, to condemn the deeds that are past and to ask forgetfulness of them from the Father, who alone of all is able to make undone what has been done, by wiping out former sins with the mercy that comes from Him and with the dew of the Spirit. "For in whatever things I find you," He says, "in these will I also judge you";[139] and at each step He proclaims the end of all

132　See Mark 2:7; Luke 5:21; 2 Corinthians 5:19.

133　See Luke 17:3–4.

134　Matthew 7:11; Luke 11:13.

135　2 Corinthians 1:3.

136　Ibid.

137　James 5:11.

138　Luke 9:62.

139　This saying, not found in our gospels, is mentioned in slightly different form by Justin Martyr who expressly attributes it to our Lord. It has some resemblance to Ezekiel 33:20 (Sept.)—"I will judge you each one in his ways""—and in both Clement and Justin it occurs in connection with teaching drawn from Ezekiel 33:10–20.

things.[140] So that even when a man has done the greatest works faithfully through life, but at the end has run on the rocks of evil, all his former labors bring him no profit, since at the turning-point of the drama he has retired from the contest; whereas he who has at first led an indifferent and careless life may, if afterwards he repents, utterly wipe out a wicked course of long continuance with the time left after his repentance. But great care is needed, just as bodies that are laboring under a long disease require treatment and special attention. Thief, do you wish to receive forgiveness? steal no more.[141] Adulterer, no longer burn.[142] Fornicator, keep pure in future. Extortioner, repay with interest. False witness, practice truth. Oath-breaker, swear no more. And repress the rest of the passions, anger, lust, grief, fear, in order that at your departure you may be found to have already become reconciled here on earth with your adversary.[143] Now it is perhaps impossible all at once to cut away passions that have grown with us, but with God's power, human supplication, the help of brethren, sincere repentance, and constant practice, success is achieved.

## The Rich Need Outspoken Advice and Warning

41. It is therefore an absolute necessity that you who are haughty and powerful and rich should appoint for yourself some man of God as trainer and pilot. Let there be at all events one whom you respect, one whom you fear, one whom

140 See 1 Peter 4:7.
141 See Ephesians 4:28.
142 See 1 Corinthians 7:9.
143 See Matthew 5:25; Luke 12:58.

you accustom yourself to listen to when he is outspoken and severe, though all the while at your service. Why, it is not good for the eyes to remain all our life-time undisciplined; they should sometimes weep and smart for the sake of better health. So, too, nothing is more destructive to the soul than incessant pleasure, the softening influence of which blinds it, if it continues obstinate against the outspoken word. Fear this man when he is angry, and be grieved when he groans; respect him when he stays his anger, and be before him in begging release from punishment. Let him spend many wakeful nights on your behalf, acting as your ambassador with God and moving the Father by the spell of constant supplications; for He does not withstand His children when they beg His mercies. And this man will beg them, if he is sincerely honored by you as an angel of God and is in nothing grieved by you, but only for you. This is unfeigned repentance. "God is not mocked,"[144] nor does He attend to empty phrases. For He alone discerns the marrow and reins of the heart; and hears those who are in the fire; and listens to those who in the whale's belly entreat Him; and is near to all believers and far from the godless unless they repent.[145]

## Story of St. John and the Robber

42. And to give you confidence, when you have thus truly repented, that there remains for you a trustworthy hope of salvation, hear a story that is no mere story, but a true account of John the apostle that has been handed down

---

144  Galatians 6:7.

145  For this sentence see Hebrews 4:12; Jeremiah 17:10; Psalms 7:9; Daniel 3; Jonah 2; Revelation 2:23.

and preserved in memory. When after the death of the tyrant he moved from the island of Patmos to Ephesus, he used to journey by request to the neighboring districts of the Gentiles, in some places to appoint bishops, in others to regulate whole churches, in others to set among the clergy some one man, it may be, of those indicated by the Spirit. He came then to one of the cities not far distant, the very name of which is told by some. After he had set the brethren at rest on other matters, last of all he looked at him who held the office of bishop, and, having noticed a strongly built youth of refined appearance and ardent spirit, he said: "This man I entrust to your care with all earnestness in the presence of the church and of Christ as witness." When the bishop accepted the trust and made every promise, the apostle once again solemnly charged and adjured him in the same words. After that he departed to Ephesus; but the presbyter took home the youth who had been handed over to him, and brought him up, made a companion of him, cherished him, and finally enlightened him by baptism. After this he relaxed his special care and guardianship, thinking that he had set over him the perfect guard, the seal of the Lord. But the youth had obtained liberty too soon. Certain idle and dissolute fellows, accustomed to evil deeds, form a ruinous companionship with him. At first they lead him on by means of costly banquets; then perhaps on their nightly expeditions for robbery they take him with them; then they urge him to join in some even greater deed. He on his part gradually became used to their life; and, like a restive and powerful horse which starts aside from the right path and takes the bit between its teeth, he rushed all the more violently because of his great nature down towards the pit. Having quite given up hope of salvation in God, he no longer meditated any slight offence, but seeing he was lost once and for all, decided to do something great and to suffer the same penalty as the rest. So he took these very men, and organized a robber band, of which he was a ready chieftain, the most violent, the most blood-thirsty, the most cruel.

Time went by, and some need having arisen the church again appeals to John, who, when he had set in order the matters for the sake of which he had come, said: "Now, bishop, return us the deposit which Christ and I together entrusted to your care in the presence and with the witness of the church over which you preside." The bishop was at first amazed, thinking he was being falsely accused about money which he had not received; and he could neither believe a charge that concerned what he did not possess nor could he disbelieve John. But when he said, "It is the youth and the soul of our brother that I demand back," the old man groaned deeply and even shed tears.

"That man," he said, "is dead."

"How and by what manner of death?"

"He is dead to God," he replied, "for he turned out a wicked and depraved man, in short a robber, and now deserting the church he has taken to the hills in company with a troop of men like himself."

The apostle, rending his clothes and with a loud groan striking his head, said: "A fine guardian of our brother's soul it was that I left! But let a horse be brought me at once, and let me have someone as a guide for the way."

Just as he was, he rode right from the very church; and when he came to the place he is captured by the robbers' sentry, not attempting to fly or to expostulate, but shouting, "I have come for this purpose; bring me to your leader." For a time the leader, armed as he was, awaited them; but when he recognized John approaching, he turned to flight, smitten with shame. Forgetful of his years John followed after him with all his strength, crying out: "Why do you fly from me, child, from your own father, from this old, unarmed man? Have pity on me, child, do not fear. You have still hopes of life, I myself will give account[146] to Christ for you. If need be, I will willingly undergo your penalty of death, as the Lord did for us. I will give my own life in payment for yours. Stand; believe; Christ has sent me."

On hearing this he at first stood still, looking down; then threw away his weapons; then trembling began to weep bitterly.[147] When the old man had come near the robber embraced him, making excuse as best he could by his groans, and being baptized a second time with his tears, hiding his right hand alone. But the apostle gave his pledge and solemn assurance that he had found pardon for him from the Savior. Kneeling down and praying, and tenderly kissing the right hand itself as having been purified by his repentance, he then brought him back to the church. There

---

146  See Hebrews 13:17.
147  See Matthew 26:75; Luke 22:62.

he interceded for him with abundant prayers, helped his struggles by continual fasting, and by manifold siren-like words laid a soothing spell upon his mind. Nor did he depart, as they say, before he had set him over the church, thus affording a great example of sincere repentance and a great token of regeneration, a trophy of a resurrection that can be seen.

When at the end of the world, the angels, radiant with joy, hymning and opening the heavens, shall receive into the celestial abodes those who truly repent;[148] and before them all the Savior Himself comes to meet him, greeting him with His right hand, offering shadowless, unceasing light, leading the way to the Father's bosom, to the eternal life, to the kingdom of heaven. In this let a man trust to the authority of God's disciples and of God their surety, to the authority of the prophecies, gospels and words of the apostles. If he dwells with these, giving ear to them and practicing their works, he will see at the very moment of his departure hence the end and proof of the doctrines. For he who here on earth admits the angel of repentance will not then repent when he leaves the body; nor will he be put to shame when he sees the Savior approaching with His own glory and heavenly host. He does not dread the fire. If, however, a man chooses to remain in his pleasures, sinning time after time, and values earthly luxury above eternal life, and turns away from the Savior when He offers forgiveness, let him no longer blame either God or wealth or his previous fall, but his own soul that will perish

---

148 This sentence, which is missing in the current translation used this book, is retrieved from ANF[2] that is translated by Wilson W.

voluntarily. But he who looks for salvation and earnestly desires it and asks for it with importunity and violence[149] shall receive the true purification and the unchanging life from the good Father who is in heaven, to whom through His Son Jesus Christ, the Lord of living and dead,[150] and through the Holy Spirit be glory, honor, might, and eternal majesty both now and for all generations and ages to come. Amen.

---

149  See Luke 11:8; Matthew 11:12.

150  See Romans 14:9.

www.ingramcontent.com/pod-product-compliance
Lightning Source LLC
Chambersburg PA
CBHW021222020426
42331CB00003B/435